# Our Final Words

Poetry from the Heart, Mind, Body and Soul

Author: Anthony Joseph Callegari Jr

# The Way of Love

## Introduction into Love

The way of love is such a beautiful and majestic way of living your life. Love comes in many different shapes, sizes, and forms it's sometime unbearable to understand. Honestly love maybe considered impossible to understand and study, yet we all can experience it within our lifetimes. Love can come within your life even when you aren't ready to comprehend it. Happiness, misery, joy, torture, creation, destruction are just a few parts of love that can occur within your mind and within your life. It can overcome the life that you hold, it can create who you are and it can destroy the very fabric of your existence as you know it. You may never comprehend its control over your mind, over your emotions, over your decisions but it shall always walk by your side once it enters your life.

The concept of a soul mate is possibly one of the most absurd concept that wonders the mind of the living or is it? To back up one end our souls are all designed specifically with a structure endlessly creating itself. We are never complete and that is why we walk this earth, to help define our souls and shape the aura that we hold. We build it through the emotion, energy, thoughts and spiritual essence that we carry. Many refer to the one we fall in love with as our soul mate by the bond we find through our similarities either by past experiences, common interests, common thought process, the situation that is present to them, failures that they create together, success they create together and the connections they make together. Some even refer to this as fate when the two paths of their lives have crossed by an unknown reason to ensure they would meet. It's a great way to believe for it gives reason to different situations that are placed in front of you, previously put into your life or possible situations that may occur but to say it is ground fact lies in your faith.

Some believe that having a defined one soul mate is impossible in a world among billions of people. Endless possibilities can occur throughout your life time and they can put you in numerous of situations that you may have never would have expected. Some call it a random occurrence that two would meet and "fall in love" together and this is based off of the concept of chaos. The concept that nothing will ever have a complete order to it and that chaos and no control shall always be reality following the idea that nothing would ever create a steady pattern of events for a certain purpose or situation to occur. It is wild to believe that this isn't true and that's when faith comes into the picture. Faith's the power to see beyond the concept of chaos and believe that situations can occur for a direct purpose within the universe. That control of events in your lifetime is possible with faith and events that could happen in a certain order for a specific purpose or situation. Faith has been around humanity for as long as humanity has been in existence and we can't prove the concept wrong but again we can't prove the concept right. Right? Many would disagree with that and that destiny, fate, love and family are key elements proving that faith is real and beliefs of the supernatural is true. Some would say that destiny is false, fate is false and to back themselves up they fall under the concept of chaos. Love they claim is a false sense of control over your mind by connecting someone else as an idol of emotion, as someone that is mentally put as a part of you without any physical connection or a person that you feel chemically pulled to from our genetics trying to get us to breed. Basically someone that connects two together by senses of emotions that they share with one another for specific reason or purpose that benefits their genetic survival or feeds the chemical reaction from the emotions that are given off. Family to them is a part of life, a group intertwined by a blood connection that shall always be related by that connection. The fact that they are created by the parents give a sense of connection that can never be broken and is a common bond for them to share and express through their lifetimes that no one else can.

Faith is a power that lies within our mind, mentally using our thoughts to believe that we have a connection through our spirit to a higher being or power and it gives many a sense of reason, a purpose within this life and a road to walk on within their own mind. Those who choose to believe differently follow the concept that we have been put her by the concept of chaos and life is just another part of the chaos of existence. We simply can't prove either wrong or right, it all follows under one another's belief in the life, love, faith, the universe, existence, purpose and everything in between.

Common faith can bring people closer within the love they create. They see it as another part of one another and it's shared as a bond. Love is undescribed and can be experienced in almost every possibility. From our minds to our bodies, from our thoughts to our souls, from our touch to our voice and through the memories we wrap emotions around for that love. Memories can be fragile if we wrap love to them which introduces happiness, joy and passion to it but if that love disappears the memory becomes a reminder of something that is gone and possibly lost forever which can introduce fear, pain, agony, loss and sorrow. Yes the negative thoughts can come even if they are still in the picture but wrapping happiness, joy and passion to a memory can shape and strengthen an existing love. It can make it stronger and intertwine those emotions closer to your mind.

Within every relationship you enter you must always look for what you want within your world for satisfying others is nice at the start but it gives false hope that a love might grow and it gives you false hope that happiness and love will "come in time". Happiness should come instantaneously and it'll start to feel unreal at the moment love enters your life. You should find joy within their presence and within who they are and how you share the time you have with one another. Love will slowly grow stronger in time and it'll require both parties to continue to try and make one another happy but never forget to hold on to your own happiness as well.

Afraid of Love? Truthfully, aren't we all? Love is scary for you are opening your heart to someone and giving them the key to your happiness and trust. It's hard for many to open their heart and let someone in mentally, physically, emotionally, psychologically and spiritually, even after they say those three words but if there is a love that has grown within both of your hearts then that trust, that love will break you free of that grasp that prevents the other to enter in and give that happiness that you deserve.

Running away from love will only make things worse in the long run for you are letting go of a love that could've been yours for all eternity to come and the thought that you burned the bridge to someone that could've unlocked your heart can be hard to even think of. That is also why it is hard to let go at times when a love has disappeared, or if you believe you and them are not right for each other. That possibility that you will lose such a chance is far too risky but yet by not letting go you are also creating a second risk of your own happiness and for that true love to come. That certainly doesn't mean all relationships hold this key but if they make you happy, truly happy and they are there for who you are and not what you are, that shall always be a perfect start.

# Emotion upon Words

## A Prayer to God

Ney be the word of God that scares you, but the mere thought of hell you fear. Keep my faith close and God closer as he'll never forsaken you. My faith within you may scar from pain and misery but God shall heal you in time. God shall and will never blink from the eyes of his glory for his eyes shall always be over you. Take his love as your light, and his heart as your road as this life shall and always will be your test of faith. Keep it strong as your head is held high to the Lord. God I thank you for this day you have brought upon us as it fills with opportunities of hope. Keep our hearts open to love and bless us all as we all thank you in return. In your glorious name, amen.

### Who we know

A mind, a body, a soul. A world upon us all, filled with tests of certainty, regret, pain, fears, hopes, and love. A challenge upon our very own minds. Determining who we are from the inside out. Let it not fool you child, but guide the mindset you withhold. Keep your mind at ease my child as this world has a plan for us all. From me to you keep it close the knowledge I shed before your ears as it'll be your stepping stone. A start to a beautiful finish. As you will always be no matter by time, never alone.

## Water under the Feet

The seas that wash upon my feet, they bring in new light to the ground I walk upon. Washing away the past and bringing in a greater perspective of a future. You never shall forget what was there, and you never want too. Keep those memories along your shore of life that you will endure, bring them to your heart on a rainy day and look into the light that glimmers between your eyes that you behold for that light shall never leave you. It shall protect your very soul and care for you with the love you so truly deserve.

### Child of God

Don't be afraid my child. Upon yonder you are brought into
this world to change, change us all! Who are they to say
words of the unspoken to your heart? Beat again my child,
show this world the light you behold. Keep it strong within
your soul and sell it to none. Blessed are you upon this world,
from the stars to earth you all are born of grace and peace.
Keep that jurisdiction close to the thoughts of us, and watch
as it settles into your mirror. Behold the child of God, a
blessing upon the universe shown between our very
own eyes. Blessed are thou among God and us all. We are
shown the light as we all are this beautiful child of God.

## Move on

Cries after lies of the truth within our youth. Misread by the light, we have forgotten our sight. Lost within our fears we grow tears of the world among us. Time passes on but can we move on? To a new light without a fright. A place to run and not hide, but stay close as if we sail on a boat. Drifting across the shores everlasting for more. Through the seas between us I'll travel far and wide to re intervene us. To hear that laugh I'll cross the borders of our land and make it back to our original plan. Confused on why, I travel to the sky. Watching the birds pass by as I lose my sense to cry. Scared of what to come for I didn't add up the sum. Not much math but more of a draft. A breeze that puts me upon my knees. Colder than the ice not even knowing what's nice. Looking back at you, wondering what's new. To look into those eyes just one more time, I'll give every breath of mine. Give me a sign just not another rhyme for I'm not worth a dime. Even by the change it's still a lot of range but just a little strange. Maybe I should move on but I can't get my groove on. I may have lost my

grip, I let it slip but I won't be whipped even if I was ripped

piece by piece, I'll slip through the grease to find my peace

once more.

## The Next World War

The guns burn our souls from the inside out. Nation raising
war against nation. We fight back for love, for peace, for
humanity. Oh the irony within those words. To strive to
come home but forsakenly left alone on the ground before
us. Our blood flows in the veins of the dead. No one will
stop us from restoring peace to a world that doesn't exist
anymore. Bullets rain like a hurricane, rising
the demons hidden in our souls. Blinded by hate we push to
kill and kill to push. Unaware of all the dying families under
our feet, we walk over each other without a glimpse of shame
but death as our last recall. Killing all that stands before us we
let the sun go down to start a new horizon. A blind of night
to our souls we are confined too. A horizon of the war of the
worlds. Another round to everlasting pain to humanity.

# The Rebirth

Fire from the undead rise to grab my hands. Binding me to death of the everlasting as I reach out to God. No voice is heard off in the distance as I stand alone in silence. Drowning in my sorrow my pain grows ever strong killing this very soul to the pits of my own demise. Scared and alone I run off into the darkness searching for the light that I have lost. Time runs ever slow along my side as the clock penetrates my ears.

The blackness covers my eyes and I become lost in the darkness to die for all eternity. Stumbling at my feet I fall. Looking at the ground before me I cry. Wondering how and why I'm here? Forsaken by my own mind, body, and soul my heart... my heart… continues to fight! Striving for another beat it forgets you, it forgets our love, and opens its eyes. It opens my eyes to God. The light shadows off into the distance as I run towards it. As the distance reaches closer, I let a piece of you go. Bigger and bigger the piece gets as I make it towards the light. With your soulless heart in my hand ever binding me to death, I look at the light glistening around the door. The voice of God then speaks out to me "My child let her go. Time will forgive her but you must forgive yourself first." As the moment wonders I break free, I drop her heart to the floor behind me as I reach for the door. A voice appears in my ears. It was her! It cry's "Wake up!" Waking up I look around. No one insight but a new day on the horizon. I knew what I needed to do. I unclenched my fist and let go of the chains binding my heart. I looked at the paper before me and after two years, I started to write again.

## The Riptides

The riptides between my heart and you sail farther and farther away. Dragging my soul away from the only known light into a world of mystery. A new and frightening understanding of a world lost between the now and the will. Yet hope still lies within my heart and I search for my one so called love. Many challenges await for this once destroyed heart. In good time let this heart heal and find a true holder for its love. Time never the less scary and full of mystery, holds potential. Who am I to be able to justify this though? A man with high hopes of love lost and destroyed in the hands of a false soul mate? A man without an inch of knowledge of where to look to find her? A man that lies between his message boards writing for a girl that doesn't exist? Well not quite truly. Writing for a girl that doesn't exist, yet.

# A Farwell to you All

A twist, a turn our road moves on. To a new start, a brand new day filled with opportunities of possibilities. We travel this beautiful everlasting road called life together as friends, as loved ones, as family, and as neighbors. One way or another our roads have passed once or twice before to connection closer as friends or foes, and yet in the end we still learn. We find our flaws and we correct them like a puzzle. Testing piece by piece to see what you can learn, to see what you can find. If our roads should departure from one another take in this, I would've never been the same man I am today without you. I cherish every moment spent even if I said a few words here and there out of regret I say to you I'm sorry. I thank you all for the time I have been given with you and I hope our days cross again. For better or worse, for today or for tomorrow hopefully one day we'll meet again. Thank you all for the time you have given to me as I hope you have a beautiful life with everlasting love and joy. Treat your love well as a trophy. A reward to someone that deserves it, not out of anger or depress but for love. Keep the connection strong and your heart stronger. I'll miss you all till the day I die and I hope we never truly leave each other. Again I say to you all thank you!

### Leaving to Chance

The life of the living built with so much meaning. Endless possibilities to all who behold this opportunity called life. Future of the unknown and the past of the forgotten. Where do we live? The present, an endless start to a life of the beholder. So many chances, so many ways. Where do we go, where do we turn? How can a simple man or women make such a decision? Is it the will of God or is it a chance we have to take? Who makes these decisions and why? Well we do. Reasons of the everlasting unknown but how can we know for sure it's the right one? We can't but it's better than letting that simple beautiful opportunity pass us by. What if it's wrong? Was it worth it? Knowledge my fellow people. It's always worth it. A lesson in time, a brighter future in mind.

## Question of Love

A world upon words. Crafted with an iron pencil, forged around our lives. We set our minds to conquer our goals and create this so called "perfect life". How can any man or women say that with confidence that they have succeeded? What a wonder though of this so called "perfect life". What can be described of it? Well sadly you can't. Well about others per say but your own, well now that's a different story. Like they say beauty is in the eyes of the beholder. Only we can truly describe our "perfect life". For many they talk of love. A word rooted in mystery but expressed by every emotion. Confided to a set of laws we create for such a word it shapes more into a jail inside of a freedom. We begin to wonder of our significant other. As curiosity begins to manipulate our mind and blind us of our love. We begin to question and ponder for hours if it's real, if it's true, if it's loyal, or if they are just using you. A scary thought, more of a nightmare if I would say. We do this for what though? For our amusement?

No. It's our trust, it's our loyalty is fault here. Once you start

to question, make sure you look back into that same mirror

first. You may find your answer.

## Pain of War

The darkness covers our eyes like the souls that pass by.
Bullets rain upon us like the fires of hell that burn beneath
our feet. But with no light within our hearts we fire back.
Giving no meaning to our sufferings like the death that
shortly follows. Our eyes tear up from the fear and pain that
dwells deep beneath our soul. Rotting us from the inside out.
Blood cries for blood as we cry for home. Our friends,
family, loved ones falling onto the floor under our feet like a
cold fall breeze. We weep and cry but fire with anger for
blood. As our minds go mind with the truth that they fire
from the same heart. Scary to believe the man we just
shot, lives now within the mirror that we look into. A dead
man with no life to give. Just a life to lose. Is it really worth
all the pain and suffering?

## Battle of a Lost Love

Within my heart I cry for you. Hours to days my soul wonders for your touch. So long and so dark I traveled to catch a glimpse of those unreal eyes. Her love was a never ending fire that burned in my heart like the battles that followed in my mind. With every grace I spent my hours writing for her. Bleeding my heart out onto the paper for her satisfaction. Giving her the love that I thought she deserved. What a fool I was to give my soul to someone without that same light. She carried her days wondering how and when. What a fine set of words she would say but for what? She would preach the words of love to my starving ears. In those simple three words that she would preach I would carry my heart into her arms. But in turn for what? For her to crush it in the eyes of the giver? By setting me out into the cold lonely silence that followed. Days turned to weeks as she won't speak. Not a word to me, but utter silence. Shattering my soul I cried for her. I would've died for her and in the end I did...

My soul and heart gave its final breathe the day she left. Time

went on and my shallow, hollow body became colder. I

wondered into the darkness in search for a light that was

blown out a long time ago. I stumbled and fell into the waters

of my own sorrow till I drowned in regret. A hand emerged

before me. The hand of God pulled me out to give me a

second chance. He didn't teach me to walk but he gave me

my first step. The step that followed by another. Till I could

walk, till I could run, till I could be free. What a pain that was

set upon my heart. Carried like the weight of a thousand

oceans, with no tide to pull me to shore. I thought I was gone

and I would never be the same. My world became her and I

lost it, left in the dark to die away. But she failed. I'm still here

and I'm stronger than ever. And I'm proud to say I can hear

that beat again.

## The Voice of the Mirror

A simple mirror, to see something clearer. Time locked between the clocks that lies over us. We look at the world as if it was a movie. Never to skip, or cut a scene. Who are we to justify this? My fellow I say hello not to bore but to see more. In you? Well in me! What I don't see is what I want to see. How the other man thinks beyond that mirror. Ask him a question, maybe two? Nothing to lose, you just need to find the clues. Like a puzzle, don't wear a muzzle. Speak to your heart and don't leave yourself in the dark.

## Our Sail

On this ship of ours, the storm brews in. Clouds cover the sky like the stars covering our night. The fog starts to take away our sun like the wind taking away our candle fire. I turn to you my love and say "My darling, I'm going to take you away from all this world that shunned you away. A place where you can finally find your peace and no one is going to get in my way of making this your reality. Not even this storm that awaits us in the night. We will make it through this darkness that lies ahead of us. Even if it takes my life with it, I promise you'll have your peace! I will never let you down, even if you fall, you'll fall into my arms!" With a smile running across your face and a hope that glimmers in your eyes, I grab the sail and head north towards the storm that cries a liquid ember colder than the eyes that we leave behind. My men with fear in their hearts turn to me and plead to turn around so we could head back, back to a so called "safety". I turn back at them and with a voice that turns a demon away I

say "Go forth on your way back to your so called "home"!
You may take the lifeboats that rest on this vessel but I'll
never turn around back to the world that tried to break our
hearts. My past is behind me and it'll stay there where it
belongs. I don't need to turn around; all I need to worry
about is what lies ahead. There will be challenges that will
break you, but you move forth and lift your head high up
against the darkness that tries to pull you under. You don't
look down and you sure as hell stand right back up! Now go
along your way and take your shame and sorrow with you!"

Not a word left their lips as they took the lifeboats and
headed back to the cold darkness that awaits them. I begin to
notice that all my crew has left me. Everybody but you my
dear. I took my head and as I looked once more at the storm
that awaits us, I cry out with love and no fear within my heart
"Look at the storm that dwells upon us. Thunder cry's not
from anger but from fear. Fear from you and I.
Determination from our love is what scares this retched
storm. Love stronger than any wave within this ocean and

our God knows this. Can this be the test from the heavens we have been waiting for? Well I know for sure, I'm not going to fail it because I won't let the love that grows with a fiery passion within your heart go out! I promised you my life, my love, and I shall keep that till the end of my last breathe!" The rain starts to slowly flow in but it quickly speeds up like an anger without a reason. I look at you and speak through my lips "I need you to quickly get into the lodge. It may be best for you to rest through the nightmare for your honor is safe with me. I'll come get you when it's all over and the storm has settled its mighty roar. I prefer you safe down their then up here waiting for the danger to take you over me. I'll be fine. My love I won't let you down!" You then look at me speechless and with a smile that shines through my soul you turn and enter the lodge. Bringing the waves upon us, the current and power gets stronger and heavier by the minute. The thunder seemed so far at first but now it seemed to close to handle. Striking the waters around us, the thunder surrounds us. Water crashes into our boat with no mercy.

Bashing us side to side without any intention in giving us a chance to breathe a single breath. The rain became far too heavy to carry and my vision started to lose its grasp through all the rain. I couldn't tell what lied ahead, all I could see was an everlasting wall of water that continued to fall as if it wanted to flood the sea. Then with a sudden bang, lightning struck behind me, throwing me down past my knees and sliding from the rain towards the end of my vessel. I quickly grabbed the railing before I was thrown off board into my own death. As I dangling from the railing, I started to pull myself up but without mercy a wave not fair behind me came over my head, with all my force I attempted to evade such a strike but I was too slow. I slipped down and hoping I'll grab back on the railing I put my hand out. Grabbing the railing I started to pull myself back up again. I lifted myself back onto the deck and ran back up towards the wheel. When I finally came returned to the wheel, I noticed something out of this world. The wheel had been struck and was beyond repair. I turned to my second and final option. I went out to the sail and started to rise it up, high above the clouds. A risk beyond the doubt with winds like this but I have no choice. I let the bag go and the sail started to rise. Wind blowing up in a whole new direction. I pulled the rope as tight as I could to guide us away from going off course but the wind was too strong to me to fight. We were heading into the unknown. The storm went on for hours on end. Winds pulling us left to right. As the storm headed off, I guided us north. As legends had it, no one could find anything north of the lands. To find land north, you would need to have found one thing first. I read that legend from a story book when I was little child. But sadly the writer never finished the last page so I could never get the chance to read the ending. But as I looked ahead of me and seen land, I noticed you walking out of that lodge and then I just knew what that one thing was that all men forget to find. Waking up I look to the mirror to face another day with a new light within my heart. A passion to carry me on to bring her a new life, a life with me.

## Key to Me

Words cannot express how my heart feels towards you, but that doesn't mean I can't pry it out of my heart. You are the only key that shall and will always unlock this rusty iron heart of mine. I finally have found the last piece to my creation and that has always been that glimmer within your eyes. You hold the key that would forever free me from this cold dark inside that has been brought upon me. My heart is forever sworn to you my key. Doubt doesn't ponder through my mind for your love serves as the beat to my heart. This I hold higher than my honor. As God as my witness I solemnly swear to you, forever I shall be yours.

### A Simple Thanks

Lord, my savior, you have sent me an Angel. A true beauty of the meaning I express through my love. Someone that has a heart pure of gold and mind that is as sharp as silver. She creates this passion that flows through my blood. I can't stand a minute without her running through the halls of my mind. She opened this sealed heart that I closed for the longest time. She holds the key now to this lonely soul and I wouldn't give it to any other. Her voice is like a flawless orchestra in an implausible harmony that breaks all boundaries. Lord I thank for your gift you have sent me and I wouldn't give her up for my dying breathe.

## Glory Justified within her

A heart as wonderful as hers only comes once in a lifetime. You're thrown off guard and on your knees and you embrace such perfection. A beauty that lies within the heart. She speaks to your soul through the words of an angel. She listens to your past and sees into your future. The love you feel from her is stronger than any foundation. Her personality is like an art show. You love everything you see … You're amazed and out of breath as you admire her every aspect. She thinks of you as you think of her. Not a negative word could be spun towards her. She's all you would ever want and more. She embraces your heart with a gentle hand and she frees your spirit with her voice. She's a diamond not in rough but on display for the whole world to admire. Whoever beholds this diamond shall and will handle with care as she is not like any other, yet far more than the world can understand. She's strong with her fight, she stands above the ground of others and can see your sins. Whoever possesses the chance to hold her close will hold heavens within their every grasp. Whoever

this man shall be I hope he knows how lucky he is for the

bond that is shared between the two would grow strong.

They shall become one and carry each other's every breath.

They shall work in sync and create a whole new world

together. They are one. They are perfect. And I only ask God

to bring them closer every day for a love like this is

something you can't even imagine.

## Trapped

I'm stuck in this cage called a classroom. It's a dungeon to me. All alone with my thoughts. Thinking about her sitting down alone and lost. The thought is eating away at my very soul and I'm stuck here…in my dungeon. It kills me from the inside out through my flesh and blood. I watch the clock as it ticks slower and slower. I wait and wait but it feels like an eternity upon my mind. I look out the window imaging her standing their cheering me on to move forward and fight threw. I wait till the clock runs out of batteries to tease these eyes of mine. I worry and worry that she's in trouble or in pain. The painful thoughts get stronger and stronger and I start to look out the window more and more often till time stands still. I know she's waiting for me but I'm not there. I pound at my jail door looking for a way out. Looking for a key. But my key is outside…waiting….for me….

## With these Hands

I had these hands locked away for longer than time can even tell. Locked away for none to see, for none to feel. The cold dusty cage I left them inside only grew darker and colder. I thought they were never going to be free, never going to be seen, never going to be touched. But then I see a light that reached out for them. I went closer and closer thinking more of it as a mirage but I was wrong. The light just got brighter and as I griped the light with these hands of mine I realized that is where I belong. The light took me with it and as I followed I didn't feel the cold darkness. The grip between my fingers grew a sense of touch as I fell deeper into the light. At that moment I knew then I would care for this light with all my everlasting beating heart. I will protect it as my own from the darkness that lived inside me. I would make it shine brighter than the sun that burned upon my head. The light then turned to me and told me her name. Lost without a word to say I held that name within my mind to cherish. The light's name happened to be just yours. A name only given to

angels sent by God himself.

# Angel

I've had an angel set upon my very life. With her broken fragile wings I shall heal her shattered soul. I shall tend to her needs and give her the chance to fly under the light once again. No matter how long it takes, I'll never rest till her heart carries a beat again. This angel is no dream, not a desire, especially no mistake but more of a miracle for my very soul. I knew the moment I laid my very eyes upon her that she was kind to this gentle heart of mine and as she smiled, she lifted this very soul set within me. Her personally and her thoughts are beyond what perfect can be dreamed of. With her brown eyes that shine like the sun in autumn, she sees into my soul and takes out my good, she holds it in her hand for the world to see. As I stand speechless and out of breath see takes my passion and shows me her heart. It was stronger than any man and brighter than any star. It makes a grown man cry and a young man to sing. I stand and with my strength I walk up to this angel that has been set forth in front of me and I take her hand. The hand was glowing with a love stronger

than I can ever imagine. I hold on and I walk through the

thick clouds of heaven along her side. As I followed her into

the welcoming light, I noticed that all I really wanted to see

was her.

## The Mask upon Me

Rules, they trap us in the cage we call perfection. Will we ever achieve such a word as our own? By truth no but by God's eyes we shall, no matter how we look behind that mirror. I thought against this idea for most of my life. It pulled me away from my true self. I felt suffocation and the constant thought that this wasn't who I was. I kept believing and following but I never got anything out, only broken promises that surrounded my past. I felt like I was chained to my conscience for all eternity to suffer in a shame to the colors that lie beyond the mirror. I felt its control over my very soul, over my very hand. I knew I was stronger… But these where only mere words. I knew I had to break free from this bind that locked me to a man I never was. I know who I am and I'm not going to hide in my mask that buries in my skin I call a conscience no longer. My conscience covered who I truly within my heart was for the longest time. What a fear set upon me, the mere thought of the mask that was cast over me. A sense of silence and loneliness haunts me; but I knew that wouldn't last for long. For God has his plan and who am I to stand in his way? For I must change, or shall let my soul be forgotten.

## The Angel's Star

Into the moon I stare. It's light shines the night sky like someone's glare. Reminds me of a beat that was created without defeat. The creator I say will never go away. I'll keep her here, without a trace of fear. Because I'll protect her even if I never meet her. She is perfect to me because I know how to set her free. She came into my life like a star but she wasn't that far. She brighten up my soul and made me whole. My heart now beats for that angel that put me to my ankles.

I'll give you a clue, that angel is you.

# Winter Flower

A flower so sweet, so small. Standing strong and tall on the hill upon us all. She waves her leaves in the wind as she looks at me. Another simple flower blowing in the wind side by side. We hold leaves and dance throughout the summer days. Fall comes as we watch the sunrise head towards the sunset. Winter blows in and as we get the cold frost setting upon us, I take my leaves over her. I cover her with the only strength I have. As the chill of the frost kill deep within my roots, I keep my ground for her. A passion grows with the thought that my other is safe within my arms. As the winter passes we hold each other close till the ice thaws. We surpass the winter and as spring sprung among us, we noticed a boy. A boy by a simply little name. He comes along and grabs us together. He takes us and gives us to a young girl. A young girl that happened to be next to him. They sat there to watch the sunset together. They hold hands as we once did and we know our love was passed on. The love they share is strong.

Stronger than a flower in the winter. They are perfect and

with their love, they are complete.

## Candle in the Moonlight

You're my candle in the moonlight, created from the starlight. Not a hint of fright flows through our night. A love so strong, nothing will stop it from caring along. But don't worry I don't bite, it's going to be alright. The wind blows but I promise never to go. Staying strong and holding on, I'm always here. For better or worse, from a letter or from a curse. Even if I start to see that light, I'll always continue to fight. From the touch of your hand to mine, it brings me to what I call cloud nine. From a smile from your face to mine, your light seems to always shine. Wings sore, like a tide on the shore. Fierce and strong, forever flowing along. Your head held high, without a tear from your eye. But what do you see, little old me. Flying in the sky, I'll never pass by. Flying parallel, never saying farewell. A love stronger than any light.  No matter how bright, nothing seems more quite

right.  Then you, my candle in the moonlight.

### Lost Touch

The darkness within your heart burns within my soul as I hold your hand to mine. The pain and suffering that burrows within your heart, tears into mine as I fall deep within your eyes. As you cut your wings and fall from grace, I reach for the light missing within you. For my hands, as much as the pain burrows within me, my hands need yours. You reach up to me for life but you ask for death as you pull me down with you. Fallen tears as I let you go from my clutches, my hands, and my life. As she falls for eternity within the darkness that lies beneath us all. Lost within the fiery pit of hell's lies, she disappears forever.

## Brother's Shoes

Death spreads like hell fire under our feet. Fighting for our life we pull the trigger. Playing a card game of lies as my enemies fit our shoes. Father time laughs at our sand falling, burrowing us within our own blood. Afraid to turn around and afraid to look ahead. Lost in a paradox of suffering and fear that chokes us till our life runs in terror of its own reflection. Our life flashes before our eyes every second of every day. Every bullet that flies by is a nightmare under our sky. A storm approaches as death knocks at our door. The chatter of footsteps that flow all around us as our enemies surround us. We fall back for cover under the laughs of our enemies. Afraid of no man but of what they possess within their hands. As we turn our heads toward the light, all we see is the end of a barrel and the shoes of our enemies. Without a stutter, my lips say their last breath, "Do it brother."

## Hands on the Moonlight

By these hands I hold yours. Under the light I look into your eyes, lost in the future I see, wondering if I'll be there. I hold her close within these arms, keeping her safe under the stars. Lying in the meadow starring at the moonlight that drags us further together. Letting the night pass us by as we fall deeper into each other's hearts. Complete silence within a thousand words that haven't been spoken. Lost within the night as time stands still, holds us along as we drift into the light among us. Each star passing by, as we watch them drift along the dark shallow sky. Lost without the words to say, we let destiny play its part. Drifting away into each other's dreams, till morning comes upon us again, to sing for a new day. For it's her eyes that I see and only see.

### Blood of the One I love

Blood sheds within my hands as I hold her within my arms. Tears rain under my breath as father time walks away. Shattered glass from her hourglass cuts through my heart. Her last breath falls into the darkness as I hold her tight; trying to hold on as she lets go. Time locked within the clock as the seconds turn to minutes. For her eyes have lost the light that guided me to her. The beauty within her soul is now paralyzed in time, slowly drifting away from my touch. I call out her name as silence becomes my answer. My heart shatters over her dead corpse, bleeding away the love I felt for her. For she was a miracle of God that left without checking out. She became my life but yet I'm still alive. Walking flesh without a soul to save her. My life, living in the past and lost in the present. I couldn't let her go for she was me. As I lie there alone in my own sorrow with her lifeless body frozen within my arms, we still had one thing together. Our hearts, as hers goes silent so shall mine.

## Last Breath

Crawling to the light that passes me by, I see your smile. Lying there as my eyes fade away with the blood of my failure within my hands. My life repeats in my mind as I lose my touch to reality. As I lie there on the ground below me, my life starts to flash more towards you. I can see your smile, I can see your eyes, and I can hear your laugh of joy as we walk the shores of life together. We hold each other's hearts tightly within our grasp as we laugh and smile about the joys of promises. I see you looking into my eyes under the sunrise till reality pulls me back. Gasping for breath as I start to feel the blood rush from within my body to the ground below me. Everything starts to turn black as I follow your voice that lies within my mind. I can see something, it comforts me but yet blinds me. It gets brighter as I hear your voice getting louder, calling my name. I reach out towards the light as everything disappears. Complete darkness surrounds me as I scream your name but all I hear though is the eco of my cries.

## Futures Lie

Time flies by like the night sky, ever growing, ever passing by. Afraid of yesterday and curious on tomorrow; yet we lose track of the present. We fall into an order of patterns that outline the road of our life. Never steering off course, never letting go of the wheel. What lies beyond the tracks we laid out before us though? Where will it lead? Father time knocks at my door as I wake up. Another day breaks in as a new start for reality appears into our hands. Yet we prepare our future by suffering in our present. Each minute blessed to us all, lost in the thought that this day maybe the day blood falls onto our hands. Till that day comes we are crying towards the sky for another minute, another beat; we take advantage of the moment, not preserving the moment that has been blessed to us all. For my heart beats for a promising future as it turns it back on the present. Keeping every beat close but eventually losing count.

## Angel of Earth

For God has sent me an angel. A blessing to say the least. She wonders the halls of my beating heart as she has become the missing piece to my soul. For I believe I already entered heaven because you have wondered into my life. For as long as we live, I will not let any day pass by our life, no minute shall leave our hands, and no moment shall escape our grasp together. For there is no time and no distance that could separate our love. Let the tide come in, I won't let you out of my sight till the day I fall under. Till the last breath of mine leaves my body, this heart will not let you go.

### The Blades between Us

By the blade falls across my eye sight. Cutting left to right as my blade draws under my waist. Across my body I feel the blood drops as it covers the floor before me with shame. I keep up and fight as my blade sheds across their skin's touch. Furiously cutting into the blood that flows through their body, I mark up the walls with red sorrow that runs through them. The pain cuts deeper than the blade but blood continues to fall cross the air between us. Fighting for more than our lives but our honor shall not be given mercy. The sharp pain cuts further than the heart can handle through us both. Holding onto the blade that falls deep across our lives we fall to the floor in unity. Watching death flow in each other's eyes as darkness surrounds our souls.

## Cut down to Hell

For my eyes need not you within sight. For the pain that follows within my soul despises you. As the sufferings of hell flow within your eyes and the fires that burns under our feet lie within the words you speak beneath your breath, I can see the pain that you hide deep within your soul. It cries out to you, yet you lend a blind eye away. You fall into the sorrows of sin as you cut your wings that you've been given. Falling from grace you look past all who give a helping hand. Suffering from your own pain that you brought upon yourself. Afraid of what might come as you suffer in the sorrow of the present that you shred through your own blood. As the red fire rains across the air you breathe, it falls to the ground below yourself as it reaches out for your soul. Walking blindly into hell fire, you suffer from your own sins for all eternity.

## The World we live in

For I stand alone within this beautifully lost world. Created by the God of the unknown and structured by the flesh that walks among us. We laugh among the common and avoid the unknown. Scarred to face the cruel reality that lies within our vision. Yet we stay in our false world created upon lies that follow us till we live under the ground we walk. Our own kind deceives and destroys each other till we fall victim from the same fate we curse upon our enemies. Yet no man nor women that laid their feet upon this earth had the opportunity to speak out what they've seen once they crossed over. For whoever gets the chance to cross, never comes back. Such a fear and curiosity that runs through our mind as we live in this world. As the tombs that we lie in cross our fate, haunt our past, curse the present we walk in, and bury our sorrows in the future that lies ahead of us, we tend to see a new light that doesn't exist beyond our own very imagination. Blinding us away from the truth that hides beyond the shadows of our own fears. Who are we to judge

our cruel reality? We are only pawns in an endless chest game

with fate.

## Perfect Poison

For my thoughts wonder and ponder with her. Yet by heart I've done wrong. For my mistakes lie buried in my past but haunts my very soul. For time shall only forgive me. She wonders the halls of my mind continuously calling for a lost soldier. Bullet scars that tears no marks upon paper but yet only upon the heart. For I know she is something more than meets the eye. Father time stands by, watching the sand fall under my feet as I continue to look further beyond the echoes of my mind. Searching for such a cure, for she has become the perfect poison.

## Feeling

This feeling that lies upon my heart, it's new to me. I never felt such a force overcome me. To my mind it's welcoming and warm. It tends to my thoughts in need and I tend to hers as well. This feeling comes over my mind as tide over the sand among the shore. Strength and courage set my body as I embrace such powers. It's a feeling that lies beyond my imagination, yet in a way I always needed. For when I'm around her, it overpowers me like the sunlight that falls into my eyes. For I don't understand such a power, yet I do not question it. For I don't know why it happens, yet why question our God of such a beautiful thing? To my heart it's an addiction without an overdose. Constantly asking, needing for more. For I must ask how such a feeling can occur? Too strong for the hands of man, I say. It's a feeling that you can't let go. For if you can control this power, the world is in your hands. A spell to say the least that overcomes the heart and controls your mind.

## Man among the River of Fish

Life, an endless river of possibilities and opportunities set
forth our journey. A beautiful mystery we have all been given.
For many they "go with the flow" but for the ones who take a
chance, bless them good fortune because they want to
become something greater. Something more than just the
average fish in a pond. They want to be the one that stands
out within our very own eyes. They want to show the world
their true colors without blinding us from the lies they create.
Make due for what they're given and create a new reality
within their own mind, within their own world. To become
someone above average and yet still swimming in the same
river among all the others. Not to flash their colors around
but to teach and create a new. A new flow within the river.
Such a beautiful way of thinking might I say to you all?

## Forsaken Me

Explain it to me! Why must you betray me? For I seen you and only you. By these hearts I stand for you not to forsaken you but to only care for you. Your eyes within mine, lost upon a world never created with kind. We had a chance for romance but you let it go without letting me know. Letting me know who you truly are, not how cruel you are. Sending me a message through a darkness by letting me deal with all your damage. For along our road you fell under but you never grew to wonder. Who I truly am, who I truly was. Why must you have forsaken me, for you have shaken me? Lost within a cold lonely world crafted by the cold lonely word, goodbye.

## Tide between our Love

The break between the tides breaks my heart. Afraid of what may come upon my soul by the light that ran away from your eyes that I once found my peace in. Afraid of the demons that lie within your mind that watches may every step. What I am, what I knew of you was gone. A world created upon beauty has turned a new cover, a new page I may say. The world has fell to ashes along the ground before us and your finger points to my words. For they were made for you out of love but used as knife against my own very heart. A mystery to say the least to me but who am I to read your mind? I'm no one to you anymore but yet you still have your blade through my heart. A pain undefined by mere words but yet my soul fights to pull it out. Push out the evil that holds the one I loved trapped in a cage. Yet I must choose. Free me or free her. A choice made by only God but yet lies within my own hands now. Torn between the lies you created and the love I once knew so deeply. For I fight for you, yet you fight against me? Asking to let go, asking to forget the love that once created the beat for this very heart of mine. What must I do? Let the riptides of our love put us together again yet no attempt is made by you. You let the waters of fire fill your lungs till you can't breathe no more, for I would give you my last breathe but that's all I can give. Forgive me my love but I must swim to shore now.

# I shall call her Angel

My angel, how I love thee. She fell in my hands with a light stronger than a thousand suns set upon the world. I was blinded by her complexion but I was shown the way by her love. She embraces my heart with a beauty far beyond what any man can understand. For the beats that lie within my heart bet faster than the air I breathe. I couldn't understand why she had chosen me but I'm just glade I've been blessed with such a gift from the heavens above. Where does such perfection come from, I may ask? Is it by the heavens or is it fate calling thou? Henceforth I shall call her my angel. Nay shall I ever call her anymore less than that for she is my light, the light that's leading my heart. The light that I will always see for she is the one I love. The one I will protect with all my heart till the ends of the earth collide with each other. The one that I'll take this long journey called life with. You're always in my prayers that flow from my soul, for within my heart you'll stay there for all eternity.

## Princess in the Tower

Along the tower ahead, you rest in your bed. Waiting along every passing night for the one to come to sight. Praying for him to find you, to help unbind you. To carry you away under the stars, and free you from your bars. Under the stars at night, came along this knight. The one that has been looking for you, so he may be renewed. To him you are his light, forever you shall be the only one in his sight. His heart beats for you, and he'll always be yours too. To climb to the top, he'll make sure he never stops. For the wind may blow, but he'll never go. For you are his entire world, his one and only pearl. He'll never stop, till he makes it to the top. For his heart belongs to you and his love shall always be true. For he'll do anything to be with you.

# My Strength for You

By the strength that I hold within my shoulders, I'll carry you across the seven seas, beyond the wildest imagination that can be created, and towards the heavens where you belong, for my words are true as the stars that follow our night sky. I shall always be along your side and within your sight, protecting your heart, your soul and of course your gorgeous smile. My hands shall only rest bound along the grasp within your fingertips. Bond to my heart and within my soul I shall forever be yours. For my heart belongs to you and I'd wait till the end of time just to see you again. Crossing the gates of hell and back would be all too worth it if it means I can hold you close to my beating heart again for my heart beats for you and only you. I've created my world around your gravity that constantly pulls me closer to your love and my hands would never pierce such a trust that lies between our words. For my strength comes from you.

## Fighting to Understand

From the swords that pierced my skin, through the cracks I fell, from the weight that became too much for me to carry, I may tumble but I shall never fall. For I search for one and one only. A play on words with the common phrase "soul mate" but yet I understand it all to clear now. As if God spoke the definition of such a word through the heart that I carry with me, for the answer was in your eyes and all that I've fought against, for every blade that sheds my skin, along the highest mountain sides I shall climb, I shall stay standing, and I shall forever continue to fight for that one. For, well,

you.

## Nature's Tide

For the tides can't separate our love. No wind can pull you from these arms of mine. I shall always hold you tight to my heart because my heart belongs to your very hands. Let no wave pull us under, for I'd give my last breath so you could breathe again. You are more than another soul wondering my life, you are a part of my life, a part of my soul, a part of my future, and the one only pearl to my ocean. You are the missing piece to the puzzle that completes me. For destiny has blessed me with you and I'm truly grateful to hold you within my arms and blessed to be able to look into your eyes and see us, see our future, our family, our forever. My heart shall forever belong to you for all eternity to come. You are everything to me and I'd give up the world that I stand under any day for you. For not the strongest tide can shift our gravity, not the brightest light can blind me from you, not the coldest night can break away our bond, nothing can take me away from you for I'll always be within your heart and I'll always be right next to you in spirit for I'll never leave your

side my one and only soul mate.

### Against the Rain

By the rain that threshes at my body, I stand tall and continue to press forth against the thunder. For my hands get tired but never weak. The rain breaks my grip over my sword but my shield shall stand higher than the stars in heavens night sky to defend you my love. For the strings that binds you and I together shall always keep me on my feet and against the wind that tries to separate our hands. For I won't let a single drop of sky fall on to you my darling, I won't let you fall under your feet, and I surely won't ever let you out of my arms. Against the world I shall stand for all eternity to defend our beautiful love, now and for all eternity.

## How my Eyes Perceive You

You are a masterpiece by the greatest divine that was chiseled by God himself. Crafted out of the finest love and sown together by the light of the Lord. You truly are the finest star within our sky and I'm honored to hold you within my grasp. For you are the amber within my heart and truly the light that shines within my life. You are more divine then any mortal women to walk the face of the earth. You to my heart, my mind, and my soul are perfect beyond all. You have always been the missing puzzle piece to me and you will forever complete me.

## My Baby Doll

Baby doll, I will never let you fall. Not a step or trip will make

me skip, even the smallest slip. For God knows how much

you glow. Like a shining star but you're not too far. For I'm

honored and blessed to hold you against my chest so you can

hear every beat, for you are far too sweet. You truly are the

other part of me and shall always be the heart of me. Eternity

I promise you, and I'll give you a clue, for everything I knew,

all I ever want is you.

## Laws of Love

My first heart beat was crafted and created the moment I looked into your eyes for truly the eyes you possess are ground shatters, I fall to my knees in amazement at their beauty as I stand side by side holding your soul close to mine, I stand by your heart forever protecting it with every ounce of my breath for by the laws of physics I am pulled to you. Drawn, maybe another word I can use but by gravity my heart rotates around you. A force uncontrolled by time and space, yet constructed and crafted by your magnificent heart. The eyes you behold shines more light than all the stars in a winter night. Truly the reason I open my eyes in the morning and why I close them at night. Yet I have lost touch with reality, for when I awake I'm still dreaming because of you. You are the light my heart follows and the hand my heart trusts. You are the only one my heart and soul desires and I wouldn't have it any other way. Back to physics, beyond my knowledge but yet expressed with you I have an attraction.

Yet we both are similar, our bond is magnetic. A pull I simply

just want to get closer to every day for my heart is yours and

truly only yours.

## Cinderella

Cinderella found a fella. Simply new but she didn't have a clue what he knew. To pass time, he sang a rhyme. For within her eyes is where he lies. To endlessly roam and make his home. For she is true beauty and certainly a cutie. I am blessed, for along her side I rest. There is no need to fright, I'll keep you alright. For it's our night and she is my light. The shores wash under our sight as we lie under the moonlight, carrying no fright within our night. For I might be right because I'm falling for her tonight.

### Deigned for you

By grace my heart creates its pace. God designed it for you

because he has always knew, from every single clue that

together we'll always make it through. My love for you is true,

bigger than the deep blue, together we grew and became

stuck like glue. Never to fall apart, for we lie within each

other's heart, creating a love that surpasses art, even from the

very start.

## Darkness in Closed Eyes

Blacker than your shadow, stronger than your fight, it comes in the night. Afraid of the unknown and betrayed by the untold. Walking within your dreams of fear, it starts to get near. Blinded by your own sight comes a stronger light. A world of the forsaken you must awaken. You are not alone for you'll be shown. The darkest shall not rise, once you see what's inside. Open your eyes and become wise with the grace of God. Give him a chance and the devil won't dance. Your shadow grows small by the light but become larger by your fright. Shall no fear show but the love of God grow, for within you'll always know, he will never be your foe.

## Angel from the Garden in Heaven

My eyes cross the fabrics of light and life to bring you into my mind, a spark of fire burns deep within the darkness of my heart to create love, a new life was created upon the world, a spark stronger than any lightning, the love that burns brighter every passing moment for you, the angel from the garden of heaven, the one who broke open the gates that have even locked me out, you brought light, fire, and a beat back into this heart I carry on this earth and you brought love to this eternal soul that walks the plans of existence. My life down on earth shall forever be yours to share, everything you are is beyond beautiful, and it's indescribable for it leaves me speechless from a single glance. You are perfect from within your mind, personality, physical body and of course your gorgeous heart. I'd give this life down on earth for you, for our eternity will forever lie in heaven.

# Destined for You

By the light that crosses through the darkest shadow that falls before me, I stand for you. I shall not betray or hurt you for you have grown and become a part of my living soul, a part of my heart and by the heavens they know it's true. My life I've wondered, searched for the one I can call my own and so she can call me her own. Not many could be given this honor, it shall only be one I say for since the start of my birth I've been destined for only one. She has found her way into my life and by God up in heaven I thank him for the one I call my soul mate. Fears may lie within each other's hearts from the past but within each other we find peace and most of all, love. An element found only within the hearts of true love and I'm blessed to have that within mine. My fears are gone, I walk this life without a single blink of an eye for I have her. You have freed me and I would never shed a single word of a lie within your heart, you have truly taken away every last fear within me. I trust you entirely and my faith is devoted to you. Thank you for being the one I can call my

own and I shall always be called yours forever.

## Blessed with Her

For my eyes have only seen one, she has become the world around me and the air I breathe. She is the light that shines over the horizon and I awaken and she is the light from the moon at night. By God's grace I was blessed with an angel of the highest divine as my soul mate, the one who truly beyond all completes me and shares within every aspect we can find.

Without a doubt I fall into her eyes that have become the home for my heart and my love. Her touch is like a spark that ignited my life. Her voice is like every beat that flows through my heart. For what did I ever do to be blessed so greatly with the one and only true love of my existence? The one that'll always be my life for I am honored to belong to her for all eternity, through every fire, through every light I shall stand by her for all existence to come.

## Bound Forever

Let the tide rise against us for our bond is stronger than any force upon the stars, letting nothing separate our arms from one another, we stand to face time itself for all eternity along each other's side. For if I must, I would give my last breath so your heart could beat again for my heart shall, always and only beat for you. Its strength is gathered by the eternal happiness within your eyes and its will to try harder and harder for your love shall always prosper over the greatest of battles for your love is far beyond any treasure. It's a blessing from God himself and my heart and soul shall always defend your honor and your love that shines forever, for you are and always will be my life down on earth and in heaven for all eternity.

## The Promise of my Life

I send you my eternity within your hands for my soul is bound to you, a world without a light brings no promises yet God brings you to prove me wrong, a light that shines over my life and gives me a reason to hold a promise to my heart and soul forever. A promise to defend a love beyond mankind, a promise to show a love beyond the tides of the world, a promise to walk through the gates of heaven. My promise is yours and it shall always belong to you my one true love that walks beside me within this life, you are the beat that flows through the veins that run through me, the breath I breathe into my soul and the light that keeps my passionate heart burning forever. My life is yours and it shall always belong to you.

## Every Passing Moment

Every moment within this life I carry it feels as if we are one

body intertwined by our love, crafted by our everlasting

passion, connected through our hearts, minds, bodies and

souls making. Our love intertwines us with a beauty beyond

all life You are the connection between reality and fantasy,

the dream that came true, the beat that started this very heart

of mine and for all eternity to come from then to the end of

now you will always be my soul mate, my love, my wife and

the eternity I will walk.

## Romeo's Lost Words

For my love shall always be blessed to you for it was created by the fires of my passion born within my heart that was ignited by you. Threw the first touch of your skin my heart made its initial beat and through the sound of your voice for which only angels could possess I found my life. My entire future within every single word falls from your lips, my love is yours forever to hold for it shall always belong to you, the light of my life and the miracle from God. You will always be my so called soul mate for destiny has brought us together as one and nothing could ever break the bound we hold within our hearts and souls. Thank you for being my life and the reason behind every single breathe I take, forever as your

Romeo.

## The Face of God

Blind with pain I see nothing, a world crafted from the fears of the past and lost in the way of the future. How can any mere mortal understand the days that pass if they hardly understand the reflection that embraces their every sight? They must see themselves as the life that they behold and the craftsmanship of God they have become. Perfection is a lie created by mankind to corrupt and destroy our passion, to rip out our hearts and burn our souls. Perfection is simply a false pretense of reality and for whoever follows behind it shall fall to their knees in their everlasting failure. It would be an endlessly journey of blind light walking towards something so divine for it represents a halo made of fire. Let not the man speak to you in the shadow you walk but yet you initiate the first step of where you may go. Your eyes must walk within the light of the Lord within the body that was shaped and designed within his eyes for he must recognize his creation for the gates to open. Let not another walker shape your mind, let not another voice guide you away, let not your

shadow take you to your knees for you are the reason life is

made, you are the face of God himself and who are you to

judge his creation?

## Glory of God

Glory I say to you God for you have created this world I walk upon, you have brought me the light for me to see and the every breath I breathe. Forsaken I shall not be for this life I carry shall always be cherished with the love and passion that my heart will hold forever, every step I walk will be away from my shadow and every path I follow will only bring me closer to your hands. My world is crafted and laid out designed by you to embrace me with challenges and tests made to create your vision of my soul. You bring me pain sorrow, misery to make me stronger and you show me love, light, happiness and joy to keep me believing in your light. Every passing moment will always be yours and every second of my world will revolve around your calling, your voice, your honor and your grace. I walk beside you and fight along with you against the evil that comes from the shadows that walk among us all. For why shall we fall when we can walk?

# A Drowning Past for a Greater Now

Are you afraid of the shadows behind you? How about the fears that walk in front of you? Does it bring sorrow of the pain you have created for the hurt you have brought? Shall not you close your eyes and run, shall not you break away from the world and fall into everlasting darkness that surrounds our pain and misery but shall you take the hand of God and accept your fate? Accept what has been done and carry on with this world for the greater good of God? You have nothing to fear but the fear you foresee in your own heart that hasn't been created yet, make light within your darkest shadows and embrace the love of God that is in each and every one of us. Make good with what you can and become the image he has always wanted you to be. Fear not the past and the pain that follows but embrace yourself for who you where, for who you are and who you should be for God shall never give up on you, only you can give up on him.

### The Pain of a Dying Soldier

My men fall to the floor under my feet in the blood of the man in their mirror. They cry out for life and fall to their death. Afraid of what's to come and lost in the life they have created. What can a mere mortal say to keep them from losing their last breathe to tears of their failure? My men look up to me but the weight of the world has gotten too heavy for them to hold, they look at me and see their own failure, their own misery. They feel as if they have let their honor down and have forsaken me? My mere words wasn't enough to convince their dying heart of the light that they have carried so far for their commanding officer, their family and their God. I lie there on the cold floor with my men, watching the world fade away within their eyes. For who am I to play God?

## The Reaper's Love

For my eyes have never crossed between the light of such

perfection till God blessed upon my world a love more

powerful than my every breath. She embraced my heart with

the glory of God within her every touch and brought to me

my life within her every word. For no man could ever mistake

her for nothing less than an angel from the gates of heaven

that rise over the light we see. She is the face of God and the

voice of angels to my everlasting soul for this world I walk on

was crafted by the heavens and shaped to bring you here. Let

my eyes see nothing more than her light and let death have

mercy upon the time I'm blessed with her for every moment,

every second I embrace by her side is an eternity of blessings

brought to me within my everlasting heart. For who am I to

deserve such a blessing into my life? A miracle of God I must

say for this heart of mine has never shown any life. My blood

has been cold for longer than life can walk. She has brought

to me fire to this lonely heart that was crafted within the cold shadows of creation. A light never seen before comes from her eyes and a love stronger than the seven seas could possibly comprehend comes from her eternal soul. Glory I say to you God for you have given death life again.

## Glory

A world of mystery still lies ahead of me for God plays no tricks and gives no hints. He walks beside us along every inch of our road, even when we banish him from our sight he walks behind our shadow to catch our every tear and hold our hand when we fall. He shows his love within the life around us, for even the smallest of good is the work of God himself. His blessing are beyond what all creation deserves yet he brings us bread and wine to carry our souls from everlasting damnation. Glory I say to you God glory.

### Devil's Play Girl

Why not you see the lies that burn in your heart? You have forsaken me beyond the point of creation to making the joy of death a pleasure to the unknown. A fear that haunts my mind as I hear the voice of evil cry from your lips and the sound of torture from the body that brings shame to God above. You show the world what evil can bring through the lies that follow from your soul. An endless blackness fills your eyes as you star back at me. You see your demise but you walk the face of the earth like a miracle of faith but yet you are nothing more than a parasite to the mind of all that follow you. You kiss the fear and intertwine your body with the torture of their minds. You walk blindly through darkness for you create it within the hearts of those who hold your hand. A monster to say the least, for the Devil knows your name and owns every letter. From the moment you took your first breathe you have given your last to him. Who do you believe would save you? Only God has that power but you have forsaken his faith, you have walked a shameful road of fire to the endless pit of torture you have created within your life. Let not the world see your true eyes for they burn in the hand of evil. Let not you see the light of day for you belong in the shadows that dare not touch you. A hell of pain you hide from, for your heart is weak and your mind is lost away from the world, from yourself.

## Meeting the Devil

Fire burns from the ground under my skin, a terrible darkness overcomes my heart as I see the face of the Devil laugh in the sight of my soul, from the moment I was given life to the moment my heart gave its last beat. He appears before me with his claws drenched in blood of the forgotten lives that came before me and he looks within my eyes. Says your faith is weak, it's false and it's gone. Blood starts to flood the ground before me, boiling from the fires under me, I look at the face of evil. His eyes black as night, his teeth sharper then the sting of a broken heart, a sense of fear that you could only smell. I look at him and shout "Our Father who aren't in heaven..." he laughs and digs his claws within my chest pulling on my heart trying to rip it out of my body and into his fires that engulf in between his teeth. I grab onto my cross and dig it into his flesh, burning his black soul from the inside out. He releases my heart and laughs. He speaks "Child of God you say, for love will never come your way, for they'll never stay, lost within their own way to my bloody claws!" I look back at him with the blood grabbing my arms pulling me under, I whisper my last words before I fall under "Hallow be thy name…" As not a moment hesitates, the blood rushes away as the Devil stands nose to nose to me, screaming "Silence you forgotten child, no one shall ever come for you!" I just continue "Thy kingdom come, thy will be done!" The darkness that surrounds me leaves with the shadows that came for my soul, the Devil starts to pull away from my sight as I speak "On earth as it is in Heaven, give us the stay our daily bread and forgive us our trespasses as we forgive those who trespass against us!" A light shines from above my sight as the fires below me start to burn out, the Devil laughs as he crawls back reaching for my chest as a vast army of shadows beyond what the moral eye can see drifts closer in the distance. I hold back every stutter and keep my faith close to my soul so he couldn't get the chance to take it. I scream with fear and faith "And lead us not into temptation but deliver us from Evil!" The Devil grabs me and pulls me into the fire, I fall burning every last inch of my body as the shadows start to

pull onto my soul, without fear I say "Amen!" At that

moment I awaken. Sweat running across my body as I look

around, nothing but darkness lies within my room. My alarm

clock turns back on and then returns to the time "1:11am". I

starred at the time for hours, the numbers wouldn't even

consider to change. I finally unplugged my clock and plugged

it back in, the time returned to normal. My mother walked in

and said good morning, I didn't even notice the time flying

by, I got up and it was Sunday. Let us just say I went to

church.

## Bringing the Beginning

Let your hope guide you away from the pain you suffer within your own heart, use the strength from God to continue to walk and his light as your breathe. You have no reason to forsaken the one who has given you life, you have no reason to question him for the tests he brings upon you, simply thank him for every second you walk along mankind for your life is merely a test from the heavens that lie far above the clouds and beyond the stars. Can you show God why you are worthy to walk in his light? Can you bring peace to shadows that follow you and can you guide a new light for your future? Let no the devil whisper sorrow, fear and pain into your heart but hold the word of God close to your everlasting soul. For this life is merely the beginning.

## Blown Out

Let my eyes not blind you from the lies within my soul, a false pretense of reality I bring to you. Who are you to wander into the footsteps of my life, can you handle the road I walk or shall you forsaken my love like the many that fallen. You are not worthy to speak to this heart for it is guarded by the pain created by lies it heard once before. A false power lies with a mere word, Love a gift of poison to the soul yet many can find peace? Burning within the past of flames and torture, lies and broken dreams. A life that was promised by a love that burnt out long before it was possible to be born. An ember of love praying to scourge into a flame yet blown out by the lies that flowed through her lips. Not even the devil could understand the fire within my heart, for God has created a light for me to follow. Broken and lost at times but I shall always carry on my way to his glory. Yet her memory still walks beside me, telling me to turn around, to look back into her eyes and walk to darkness promising eternal love.

Shall I not fall into the shadows, I merely rather walk towards

God with a broken heart then to lie in darkness holding onto

a love I can't see. Can you be the one to break me free, can

you show me the way to walk for even I'm lost upon my

road.

## Carrying God's Message

By the light that flows through my everlasting soul, I bring to the heavens a love stronger than mankind's heart. I have not and shall not forsake such a love to you God for you are the single greatest blessing to all existence, you are the breath that flows through the body I possess and you shall always be the reason for life to wonder through time. Let not possession take away what is given in spirit, let not the lies of the world take away the light within my eyes for God will always carry me but I must be the one to walk. I must be the one too talk, keep the faith within my words and my actions that I bring to this world. Carry out God's message through the hands I write, through the words I speak, through the heart that beats, I carry out your message, I will fly through the paper that is brought before you and I shall keep the ink stronger than the flames of evil. For this life of mine belongs to you God.

## Your Shadow

The shadows haunt the everlasting soul you carry, following behind your every step for once night comes the terror of evil haunts your dream. No sword, no shield from the torture your mind carries but yet God awaits for your belief, can you understand the power that you behold? Can you save the life you carry and fight off your demons with a faith you have long forgotten? Let it be known by every passing second the demons that haunt your dreams walk among the shadows closer and closer to your heart, to one day rip it from the body you hold, to tear apart your everlasting soul. A fear among the life span of existence but you carry out your days forsaking your Father in heaven. Questioning his existence and his love. For he reaches out for you no matter the words you say, the life you betray, or the world you walk away from.

Keep in mind it is never over, till you say so.

## The Blind Man's World

By the blind man I walk beside him, he takes me to a place where only he can see. A world beyond any other, with a fabric of creation wilder than the forests of the earth. The trees grow beyond the sky, the water flows perfectly north and the tides are as calm as his voice. He talks of peace without bloodshed, he talks of order with a sense of control and he talks of nature has a part of humanity not as a slave to our terror. Words of such beauty speaks from his mind, heart and soul, words describing perfection on this earth and a love that spreads across the seven seas into the hearts of all the living. No fear comes to mind to any form of life, no shadows walk behind our every footstep and no value to the air we breathe. He talks of passion, creation and imagination of the world set not in stone but within his mind, a world he hopes to see one day when he wakes up.

## Not even in my Dreams

She runs into my arms with the cutest charms, delightful with spirit without any fear in it. Such a child fun and wild lost within her imagination larger than any nation. A beauty beyond the world and a cutie beyond her twirls. The mother, my wife so full of life. She makes my day and holds my night between every flight. From the stars at night to my closest light, she'll be there. I always thought we'll go far but I never seen the scar. Her heart beyond my reach and her art beyond anything I can teach. I try to preach my love but I would always be shoved. I written it within my sorrow for she'll be gone tomorrow. I want her to take me but it always wakes me. My dreams don't last long and then they're gone. Each night it takes longer to make it stronger. Broken and gone I stay and continue to fight on. But even in my dreams it seems she disappeared, we never feared of a day when it'll wash away. Who would have thought I would be caught and brought back into reality? To a world without you for what can I do I have no clue how to make it through and bring the

number back to two. Can't I lie here forever, it may be very

clever but I know it'll be never. For I have this life, it may be

without my wife but that doesn't mean I bring out the knife

for who knows if they'll be an afterlife for a man like me?

# A Dying Soldier's Heart

Bullets struck my armor, breaking into my soul. Shattering the very fabric of my existence. Lost without a word to say, I stumble to the floor that I used to walk on. Reality speaks no more for me and time starts to move faster than my eyes can handle. My men caught under the choke of their own blood from the lead that flows in the air, fall beside me. I look into their soulless eyes and see my future that lies not too far from now. Every emotion rushes my mind and all I can see is you. The woman I love running into my arms, tears rushing down your face as I caught every one with those simple three words. Just like my soon reality that beautiful love has been gone. That woman that owns every ounce of blood within my heart disappeared from my existence. Walked out of my life without a fight. Wandering the world as I'm lost within my own sorrow. I shack back into reality from the voice of my men. Speaking words of how they'll make sure I make it home. I laugh under my breathe knowing my world is gone, there is nothing left for me to go home too. I look back at him as blood rains upon me like the heaven's crying. He falls on top of my flesh as his eyes speak no more. I push myself up as lead fills my body tumbling me down to the floor below my everlasting soul. Unable to move I look up and I see her. Beauty beyond all existence and a smile that brings me new life. I look closer and the barrel fires. My last words that belonged to her, didn't even have a chance to speak.

## She Loves Me Not

A lie set on stage. Played like a drunk at a casino and tricked like a magician's audience. My love broken out of the chains of my heart and wrapped into your arms with my blessing. My love is all I have and it belongs to you. Dropped like a bad habit I was gone, disappeared from her reality. Not another word heard, not another spoken. Lost like the wind, my heart was scattered like the ocean. Like a child she was afraid to step in, to feel the coast rush under her feet. It was there for her and only her, a place built around the fabric of her existence designed with every last beat of my heart. She wouldn't even touch the sand but walked away like her eyes saw a storm in the distance. My heart bound to her existence was lost without directions, no map, no way in and no way out. I was gone, broken to the point of molecules. Our lines crossed beautifully, with a passion beyond the angels' imagination but like any lines that cross they'll pass and continue to create distance over time. I reached out for her but I fell off the grid, falling to hold her one last time. She couldn't see me, she never looked back. I fell into the darkness that surrounded my existence and drove off the road I called life. Fear, pain and sorrow guided me away from the light but God's voice just got loader. Something even in death you could hear. I followed his voice but my legs where weak and my heart was weaker. I couldn't stand life without her, I couldn't stand without the other half of me. I woke up again, another nightmare, another fear and the words that only came to my mind, "She loves me not".

### The Curve

We were perfect like parallel lines but we never got close enough to touch. Our hands reached for one another but we could never grasp onto the hearts that sung each other's name. We wondered the stars side by side, asking, pleading for a single moment to cross, to hold one another close so we may have a change to never let go. Who would have thought that day would come, she took the curve but it wasn't to me. Her eyes wondered from my sight and my voice got loader and loader for her name but it just got quitter and quitter. And all I could think about was that she had the chance, she had the power but she went the other way.

# Her Last Words

Shattered like the glass of my heart, your eyes tear up with only two words "I'm sorry". To forever be the last words engraved into my mind from your lips, broken and alone my soul lost its grip, you walk away and all I can follow to make it back to you was the river of tears that you shed for me. It must have been a drought for I lost the path all too soon, you wake up in the morning with a smile of a new day as I come to realize the night passed by without a single moment for my eyes to rest. You watch your future role with imagination of beauty as I'm lost in the past, wondering for a glimpse of you. How can I wake up if my eyes never close? How can I speak of love when love has betrayed me? How can I walk another step without the other half of me? By the Lord's hand I'm given strength, surviving off the Lord's Prayer I breathe. Not a day wonders my life without a moment of silence for you but those days are gone, that life, that world is falling apart within my mind and my grasp has been lost. All I ask for is another word, another chance to hear that voice call my name

again. Simply though who am I?

# Freeing my Heart

Let my heart beat again! Pleading I am to you for my heart is shattered and stuck by the lonesome silence. Break me free from the chains and walls I built around my everlasting soul for I am lost and blind within the darkness. My light disappeared from my heart and my life. She wondered away in silence without a chance for a goodbye. Her voice is just a mere memory like the idea of light to shine back into these eyes I carry. Let not my soul and love be forever trapped within these walls for they have a key. I don't hold it, I got no grasp upon anything for there is nothing to hold. Only love can set me free again, give me a breath to breathe again. My shadows I can feel surround my presence, I can hear there silent laugh and the voice of darkness call my name asking for my heart. I shall never fall to their knees but rather die within the lonely depths of my heart. The cold shattering wind that rushes between me breaks my hold on reality. The blinding sorrow that echoes within the air shuts my eyes from the days that pass by. Who am I to be free? A Romeo without a Juliet

I may say for love is my only key, it is all I know, it is all I

breathe and it will be the last thing I hold for it is all I want to

hold.

### Creation in your Blind Eyes

By the God's light I shine a new horizon. A new view upon the reality I walk, a world beyond any other created from the fabrics of time. A new day with a light blinding the eyes I behold setting forth a beauty for which my eyes could never understand. Can you see the light your heart brings to you? Can you understand the words spoken by the voice of your soul? Is it your destiny to walk the road you have chosen or is it fate that wants you to understand the fabrics of creation? Can you see that life has no end but a dead line for its trial. This world is merely the beginning, the point in life where you choose your side, your fate, your life. Why can't you see that reality is merely a false pretense of creation, designed to test your very soul of emotions, fear and power. Simply I say

Amen.

## Not in my Stars

The shadows of my past wonder under the light. Haunting my dreams and hiding under my bed. My love shattered from reality and broken by the truth. Recreated by the light of the Lord but still lost for her. She wonders in the darkness, hides in my shadow, she is the very reason my love fears its own reflection. How could I say goodbye to forever, how could I find her again? She disappeared from my grasp and even the eyes I possess walk the darkness looking for her, yet no light comes within my sight. Not a star wonders my night and I know what I hold dear to my heart is lost upon the stars I can't see. She is the comet that crosses my world but like a falling star, you only see her once.

## Forgive my Heart

Forgive my love Father for it has been shattered again. Broken apart and scattered across reality and my dreams. You God will always have my love but for the light to cast on another, I will be blind to say I do. She doesn't exist within my heart and has disappeared from my dreams. She cast a plague to my hopes and set fire to my trust. Walls higher than the eyes could possibly fathom and bridges crumbled under the shadows of creation. She may walk upon this earth but she doesn't walk in my dreams. She is a ghost, a false pretense of reality that falsely appears within my mind. My imagination shall not create up another lie, another heart break, another mistake. It shall not create an image I can't hold for I won't let it. My heart is too weak to understand love anymore, it needs a helping hand but sadly I'm all alone.

## Depression

Run, run before the wolf comes. Before light turns to night filled with frights.

Lock the door before you can't sleep evermore. Jump into the bed before it is said.

The words echo outside "Find them! Find them! Then blind them!"

"Who to see, nothing to flee, we are like a tree, don't you agree?"

Close your eyes for it is inside, in the walls and across the hall, under your bed and in your head.

What can it be, well let me see? Ask your mind and you will find the answer but we also seem like a dancer, ever moving, ever proving that we aren't losing but choosing.

Choosing who, well how about you! Oh why, don't cry, we aren't going to lie.

We are here, not to cheer but to see tears.

To hear your cries with your eyes, to find your lies without

your ties.

Do we go? Oh no. Can you fight? Yeah right! You need your

light but its night.

## Loneliness

Cold and dark silence fills the room. No light in sight within my eyes or within my mind. Afraid of tomorrow and lost in yesterday, I see a glimpse of you. Beauty beyond all existence can understand, yet lost within a memory that fades by every passing moment. The fires that burn our love grows dimmer by the day and the waters that I walked along side you have made a tide from the storm that brought us apart. Pain floods my soul as sorrow wonders every corner of my mind. How I wish to reach back to you yet you cut the cord, you broke the chains that bound us together and now they strangle my every breath. A poison rushes through my veins and I hold onto our love. We were a star, the brightest of them all, yet we burned out like a candle. Blown away like the wind between us and all I have left of you is an echo.

## Blind Love

For even if I'm blind I can still see you. A beauty beyond all the world, seen through the eyes of your voice and captures by the beat of your heart. A rhyme beyond any melody can comprehend, a tonality beyond description and a musical form beyond any other. Let my eyes be within my touch and your heart be within your kiss. Let your eyes shut and my voice be your guide through this life. Let my heart be your voice to follow and my soul as the hand you carry. Let not the world set fear into you, let not your eyes open for the night has just begun.

### Foundation of Reality within Her

Let the fires burn faster than the engine within my heart for nothing can stop me! I'm beyond my own control and my brakes are shot! Lost upon my own imagination I create you, a figment of my future and a reality not present upon this earth yet but my passion bring me to reach beyond the planes of existence. I wonder between both worlds to bring you here within my arms, I cross the seven seas of my mind to craft you within my imagination and break your heart so I may reshape it again! Let not fear drive you away for you may not escape my grasp, let not the world tempt you from my eyes for they are yours to behold forever, lost within my reality you shall rest in peace for all eternity.

## Just the Start

Once you rest your soul within my hands I will shelter it with the heart that I forged within our love. Let not the words of the world scare you for no fear lies within my eyes. Beyond the universe and all existence you rest within my arms to hold back time from stealing a single second away, for forever shall only be the start to our adventure but first, I need to find you.

## The Apple of our World

For my eyes are lost upon a world forgotten centuries ago, a world no mortal walks anymore, a spirit world full of passion, a world wondering with love and grace, peace and harmony, trust and the possibility of forever, who would have though our world could lose such a beauty. A vast wasteland of sorrow and shattered glass from one another's hearts we walk upon. A world destroyed by creation and lost without imagination. We live in a world overcome by fear and mistaken for courage. Our lives are no more important than the souls we rest beside so why step over them like a fault in reality, as if they were made to be a mistake written by the words of God. Sadly though God watches but his hand can't control us for we took the first bit.

### Honored for Her

Gravity couldn't even define how my heart is pulled towards her, she is the every single heart beat that follows through my veins, the voice in the halls of my mind that echoes endlessly like a beautiful melody that you never want to leave, the light that shines within my soul beyond what my eyes can handle and the love that burns within me like a fiery passion brighter than any sun. She is God's greatest blessing and I'm honored to have her love for she has all of mine.

## Hope within Destiny

For my heart, bound to the chains that protect it, pray for a
key but only time shall tell though. But who am I to question
destiny? Let I not be foolish and let my heart not be forsaken
again but I know I can't be this way forever. For she may
come. All I need is hope.

## The Devil

By the fires within my heart the eyes you behold speak no truth to my restless soul. I can see within your lies a world of sorrow and darkness, founded upon the evils of your creation. Your hands cold as the fires of hell, draw closer to mine but I shall not fall under your spell, under your eyes that curse the name of heaven and talk to my demons. You are no mortal but again not immortal, simply you are the face of darkness and dread that haunts the minds of the living. You create pain upon their wildest nightmares and walk alongside their fears. But I know who you are, I know you are simply alone without passion, without love, without eyes to fall back into yours. You are alone and you shall always be for all eternity.

### The Shadow within my Heart

The darkness surrounds my everlasting soul with a pain trembling in my heart. My shadow has overcome my steps and I now am forced to follow it but even my shadow fears the dark sea of my heart. I wonder alone across this life without love to hold within my heart, within my soul, within my mind. I wonder endlessly through the emptiness that surrounds me, continuously till my last breathe. For who I am to breathe the air God has blessed to this earth? Who am I at all?

## Dead End

Lost within the darkness around me I call out for an answer. I call out for forgiveness, I call out for love. All I ever get in return is silence! Not a word, not a sound, not a shred of light to pass through my heart, just mere sorrow and pain. Lost and alone I walk this road coming upon the end I look ahead, trees as far as the eye can see but no life in sight. The leaves have vanished from the forest and only dirt is set upon the ground ahead of me. I stand upon the ground as I look back, all I can see within my sight is the darkness that has followed me, the darkness that calls to me within my dreams. Not with mere words but with silence, a silence that breaks my heart. I leave the road I walk for I've hit the end of the line. Nowhere else to wonder but the cold dreadful dirt upon the forest that lies ahead of me. May I not ask if it ends for I know the answer. May I not question the trees for they are long gone without any words to say? Merely I must walk till I find light again but I still wonder if it'll only be another dead end again.

## Dying Heart

For my heart would give anything for its beat again. A chance to live, a chance to see light flow through the eyes of an angel once more. To hear a voice call forth my name and without a hesitation hold on to me, to never let go no matter the storm that may follow. My heart, tired and unrested calls for an end, calls for complete silence. Yet I know the only cure is within the eyes of another mortal. Another that could save my dying heart from everlasting pain and torture. My heart from an eternity of sorrow and dread. Just to hear another voice I ask for, something to give it hope.

## The Chains

Free me from the chains you bind against me, from the flames you have pulled underneath me. Free my everlasting soul from the sorrow it has drowned upon. Hold me within your arms and talk words of forgiveness, talk words of passion, talk words of love. Speak to me once more and end this silence that wonders the halls of my mind. Free me from the pain that I endure within the rooms I walk towards. From the memories to the emotions, from the passion to the love, all have become a poison upon my mind. All have become the chains that bind me.

## Spread to my Dreams

It haunts the halls of my mind, torturing my memories and poisoning my thoughts. Darkness over shadows my soul as my heart falls under the grasp of her claws. She draws me in through her voice and intertwines her fingertips with the strings of my heart. She rips me from the body I hold and claws into my soul. The light within me bursts me free from her grasp but my heart falls under the poison it lies upon. Burning me from the inside out, constantly being tortured by the silence within my mind, dread compels my mind to fall into darkness and I shut myself out. Locking the door and tossing the key into the darkness beyond my own control, the chains wrap around me like death knocking on my door. She calls for my name but I speak of no name, I wonder lost but the chains hold me back, they drag me under and the shadows that surround me torture my everlasting soul into the fiery pit of fear that my mind has created. I wake up, alone upon my bed. Someone knocks on my door and all I

hear is my name.

## Still within my Dreams

You're never alone I tell you, hold on to me for my life is yours. Her eyes fall back into mine as all I hear is goodbye. The shadows take her into the darkness that surrounded us and silence fills the air. I scream for her name but the still silence brings a laughter to me. Haunting me and torturing me of those words, goodbye. Screaming it silently into my soul forcing me to hear it every waking moment I breathe. My only escape has been my dreams, my world created upon my hopes but the darkness has followed me, it has trapped itself within my mind and came for me. It laughs again silently as the light dissipates into the sorrow eternity I walk. Every dream has its poison and nightmares follow my shadows. I'm lost and they found me.

## Second Chance

My suffering heart lost and broken in the flames of sorrow,

betrayed by the last love it can endure has forgiven you. It has

forgiven your touch, your voice, your lies, it is free from the

chains it hanged itself from. It walked alone so long within

the darkness I've created within my own mentality of love but

I've been freed. By glory of God's mercy he has freed me

from my sorrows and given me another chance to breathe. I

open my eyes to a new day wondering aimlessly into the light

that I've been given. Forgive me Father for my darkness

walks behind me within my shadows but I know its name and

I'll never forget it again. Let my heart beat for a love once

more and let my voice prove its faith through your words of

wisdom. For my life is yours and that shall never change for

even at night with you I can see.

## Come Forth and Strike!

Fight me my angel, strike my heart with your poison you rest within your soul for I shall not die. I'm beyond the power of the heavens that wonder above the sky, I'm beyond the fury that lies within your sword which rests in your hands, so strike me! Stutter under your breath, you have no chance against me! My heart shall not die, not as long as I stand willingly along its side. Damaged and broken from each heart beat, every broken piece of glass that wondered from my grasp, no matter the pain I continue on my journey among this life for I have no fear! Simply I ask strike me! I'm fearless, I'm not lost, I'm beyond my own power, I found myself now so you have no control over me anymore. So come at me with all the might you carry for even at night I now have become your nightmare!

## Amen

Don't be blind my child show faith within what you cannot see. It lies within your heart and wonders within your spirit. Its power is beyond all creation for nothing rises above it. Be not afraid of what you don't understand, embrace the beauty within your heart and within your mind for his words are a blessing. From the touch of his grace he brought your life and with the power resting within his hands he can wipe the face of the earth dry of the soul within the devil. He looks at you as no mistake but a masterpiece worthy of every breath taken. Let not the souls that stand beside you wonder your eyes away, let not the touch of skin drive you under the water to drown but let your faith guild you past all disbelief. In his good name I say amen to you all.

# President's Speech to God

Burn me at the cross at the hands of mercy. Free my soul of the terror that walks upon my life. See my soul for the beauty it possesses and not the fear it adheres in its mind. Free the blind of the darkness that walks within their mind and bring the deaf their chance to hear your voice. Reality is false compared to the heavens constructed within our hearts and the imagination shaped by our lies. Who am I to command such authority over the world, over the ears of the little, over the hearts of the broken? Why do I walk side by side with the Gods of the living but breathe simply the same? Let the secrets unfold from the lost and the oceans open up to free their curiosity. Let my borders burn at the hands of justice and the swords fall to your name. Let the last drop of blood end with the resurrection of your son and peace run wild within the grace we live by. Free us of the evils we have become and cast our sins to the fires of hell. Let our hearts be reborn in your favor, this I simply say. Amen.

# Quotes

❧ For even if I'm blind I can still see you.

❧ You say to me "Where have you been all my life?" And quickly, without a hesitation I'll say "Looking for you!"

❧ To be honest I rather live a perfectly beautiful life with my soul mate than a perfectly successful life with myself.

❧ Society is so caught up in money when in the end you work so hard to make a life that you forget to live your life! Let's live our lives that we possess and stop looking at the money aspect because all you are then is another cog in the system and that is what they want you to be! They don't want you to have a voice, well it's your time to speak!

✤ Let my heart be pierced by your sword for my heart will only bend your blade.

✤ Sometimes people just need to understand that they might be looking in the wrong place.

✤ Sometimes it's hard when you keep cutting yourself on the broken glass of your heart as you try to repair it but someone has to fix it.

✤ I would shatter my world to keep her heart safe and I believe I did, God picked up my pieces but I have to put them back together.

❧ The sense of worthiness over another is falsified. Love is a powerful element that will alter your reality and once lost, even for the right or wrong reasons still can make you feel as if the blame is on you. Nothing could be farther from the truth. Everyone deserves true happiness and love, a sense of completion within the touch of one another's arms. No mere mortal is worth more than anyone else, not even through the eyes of love. Yet they can be blinding, remember we are all built equally and designed uniquely. Simply keep faith and look only in the future for if you wonder with your eyes in the past how do you know where you are heading?

❧ To free your heart, you must free your mind. Let go of the world and vanish from your own mentally to see yourself truly within that mirror. At that point you will be able to ask yourself the questions you always wanted too. Don't be afraid of being alone, you are never alone, God is simply testing your strength of mind to surpass a need to have someone within your life to hold a happiness. You are not alone trust me.

✤ The lone wolf dies forgotten but his words will never fade.

✤ Let not your heart guide your mind and let not your mind guide your heart for that war is beyond creation.

✤ Open your eyes child, even if you fly into the shadows of sorrow only you can find your way out.

❧ For my eyes have seen your evil alongside your angels, I am not blind nor foolish but my heart speaks of no past, no present, only a future.

❧ Let the fires within your heart be your fuel not your demise!

❧ For your world shall cross many seas, don't drown in the shallow waters of emotion, build a boat from your heart not someone else's.

❧ For my heart beats but does it give a sound?

❧ To all the woman who fall under the mental mindset that they are just a "figure" within society and that you are nothing more than an object, you are clearly wrong, you are temple, a masterpiece of God himself designed on this earth like any other woman, like any other man, like any other human. We are all equal and should be viewed equally through the eyes we possess but many fall under the selfish vision of judgment. Love is by the sight of heart not the sight of complexion. You are beautiful inside and out, your heart and soul are the foundation of creation and for you to idolize your body over anything is completely falsified. Your soul, who you are and what you believe comes before anything for no one could ever compare to the one and only YOU! You are designed perfectly in God's eyes as a masterpiece of creation from the start, every so called "flaw" was put onto you to test your strength to see the true beauty in you and to look past that mirror for God knows exactly what he sees. He sees you, do you?

🐺 For my eyes are not blind or mislead, just precautious and focused.

🐺 For my heart shall wonder eternity no matter the road it follows to find you, for you shall always be worth every last step.

🐺 The lone wolf is always forgotten but not his words...

🐺 For my heart loves too much, my body tries too hard, my soul believes too often, my passion becomes too strong and my mind trusts too soon, so it's up to my conscience to protect them all and show them reality.

🐺 Question not the life you've lived for you are made to learn and understand, feel and master pain, love, torture, fear, joy, sorrow and every emotion in between.

🕊 For this life is beyond all others, a chance for God to see if we are worthy of the heavens we pray for. He walks beside us, silent at times to see if we can hold our faith even through pain, torture, sadness and guilt. For he knows this life is only temporary but the heavens are eternity.

🕊 For the eyes of the living will see a light within every lifetime, it is God calling out to us, showing us that heaven awaits for our arrival but time holds our hand along the way, teaching us how to handle such an honor with every laugh, every tear, every accomplishment, every loss and within every step we make. God tests the ones he believes in the most so if you believe your life is cursed, maybe it's God testing you even harder for he believes in you a little bit more than everyone else.

🕈 The goal is not marriage, it's an eternity filled with love.

🕈 Every man can be a Romeo and every women can be a Juliet, just don't drink the poison.

🕈 Every day, every single day is a gift from God not a curse.

🕈 Never be afraid of the face that lies ahead, even if it's your own for God has brought this world to you as a test of faith, devotion, respect, honor and love. He who walks with God will run with God, he who walks

away from God runs away from God. Let your lies

not blind you but your truth guide you.

Time doesn't matter, it's what you do in that time that

does.

Love is more than mere words, it's something that

can't be explained, not even taught. It's something

that grows within your heart that crosses all

boundaries. It breaks down the walls that suffocates

your heart and it gives its last breath so you can

breathe again. You want nothing more than to make

them truly happy and you never want to stop finding

ways to express that love. They do more than enter

your life and make you complete, they become your

life and all you ever want to do is be by their side,

holding them close, protecting, caring and loving them forever. Within their eyes you see more than a reflection, you see your entire world, your entire future with them, you see every amazing moment that you'll share with them for all eternity and it plays over and over again within their eyes. It's truly beautiful when you fall into their eyes and make them your home forever. For within your eyes all that you could ever see and imagine is them. Love is truly the most amazing feeling that could ever happen to you for they become your entire life.

 

&#9753; Just remember, the impossible is possible.

 

&#9753; A picture speaks a thousand words but a thousand words show a picture.

✤ Life, an endless river of possibilities and opportunities set forth our journey. A beautiful mystery we have all been given. For many they "go with the flow" but for the ones who take a chance, bless them good fortune because they want to become something greater. Something more than just the average fish in a pond. They want to be the one that stands out. They want to show the world their true colors. Such a beautiful way of thinking might I say?

✤ For she is no mystery, she's an angel.

✤ Don't be afraid. You have nothing to be ashamed of. For it's your past and it's designed to stay there. It's crafted to teach you. Whatever you do remember it's the present now.

✤ For the fears that lie within your heart live under your bed. A scary truth that blinds us from reality. What a thought but as it stands, it only lives in our mind. A battle with ourselves that crosses the border of reality. No need to fear though child, it isn't real.

✤ For the voice that lives within your soul speaks no lie; do you have the courage and strength to listen and fight your demons? Keep your heart strong, your mind stronger, and your faith above all for you may only get that one chance. Don't let it slip away.

✤ Follow your mind and guide with your heart. Don't mix them two up. For if my soul carries no weight, do I exist?

❧ For my life carries over no other. Let my hand cross no blade over yours but let your mind not overcome you. For the cut would blind you from the life you behold if you cross my line.

❧ We are all born equal, men, women, and child. Who are we to judge another? Who are we to tell if they are doing the right thing for themselves? Who are we to dictate someone else's life? Is ours so perfect that we are given this right? Yes we may know more here and there on basic knowledge but what about emotion? Who are we to say they aren't in love? Who are we to say that he isn't right for her? Who are we to separate them? Why are so many people given such a mentality? Is it selfishness, guilt, jealously? In my eyes it seems like power. What a sad face of reality but to some it's their mentality. A rhyme, maybe so but that isn't the goal. It's to teach, not preach. Words unspoken from one another, blinding us from our true lover.

🦋 My fellow people I'm blessed to have you all within my life and no matter these eyes will never hide, yet it'll look back into yours with open arms. A life of an open book shall always be in your grasps. Secrets are made to blind, as truth is made to guide.

🦋 You know what I hate, I hate when someone tells you "You're too good for me". Really? How could anyone be "too good" for someone? We all are born equal with a blessed heart and soul. People make mistakes, we all live with them. So why look at yourself lesser for that? When I'm told this I feel as if they are emotionally unstable and that they say they aren't worth it. Why do you think I'm with you? It's because I think you are worth it. Now not everyone feels or expresses that in their heart when they say this but to me it feels that way. I personally can't stand it because it shows that you are making yourself mentally weak by hurting yourself because you think they deserve better. We are all equal. Plain and simple. No one can be better than another. I don't know, maybe it's just me. Enjoy your beautiful lives, and remember that no matter what, you are beautiful and worth every second.

The importance of marriage is falsified. Marriage should never define a relationship and should never become a factor if someone is right for you. Marriage is a common belief practiced by many for the sense and feeling of a true bound connection between one another. Marriage is simply a lie that keeps both parties false trust in one another. If you truly love someone, that bond that you share should always feel everlasting and feel stronger than any paper could say. In my perspective avoid the thought of marriage as your goal but love instead.

&#x266B; Remember this life is temporary, nothing comes along with you for the ride to heaven or hell so ensure you do all that you can in this life to do right so you may have the chance to enter heaven above.

&#x266B; Let your purpose within this life to always be to find true love and happiness for once the day comes where you pass along to the other side, you and them shall be the only thing that makes it across.

&#x266B; It'll always be a never ending battle between your heart and mind, a war upon creation shifted by imagination. Find peace not in the moment but your

reality. Create a life filled with moments, not a single

moment to define your life.

*Author*

Hello my fellow people. My name is **Anthony Joseph Callegari Junior**. Writing is more of an art within my mind and even though it may not fall under my major within my studies it has always been a powerful passion I hold and improve on over time. My passion for writing falls back to my first love, she brought out the words and spun them within my heart. After her departure my foundation was gone but my passion kept me standing. I have become the pillars that hold me up and I reinforced them with my every heartbeat. Through all the storms, every battle, every war; my family, my friends, my love ones have always been the crutch to my survival. Now I have prospered beyond my own powers and become self-sufficient within my own mind, body and soul. No matter what I am forever grateful for the love I have been blessed with from my family, friends and love ones. So simply thank you.

This book is designed to be a collection of my emotions spun into words written for you all to see how my heart beats. Its purpose is to express the words my heart has spoken and inspire you all to find yourselves, who you all belong with, to see the power love can do for you and to understand my view upon love and life. To me love is a crazy word, rooted within our hearts and structured in our minds. We look so hard to find that connection with someone other than the reflection that lives within the mirror but the question is how do we find this so called love? Well love is a connection that sparks by a touch, a feel, a look, a breath, a thought. A connection that breaks all boundaries and pulls you to who they are, not what they are. A connection that blinds your eyes but opens your heart. Love isn't based upon the looks but the feel, the connection, the comfort that you can close your eyes and still see them. The joy that you can only get by being with them. This love is truly beautiful and I am grateful to have been given the chance to experience its beauty. Yet they have gone, swept away like the wind I am thankful, thankful for the time, memories and knowledge brought to me. Forever they'll live in my heart and memories. Just don't forget to look ahead, for if you wonder your eyes in the past, how can you see your future?

*Dated: October, 2016*

*Age: 20*